MY CANADA

BRITISH COLUMBIA

Weigl

Published by Weigl Educational Publishers Limited
6325 10th Street SE
Calgary, Alberta T2H 2Z9

Website: www.weigl.ca

Library and Archives Canada Cataloguing in Publication

Goldsworthy, Kaite, author
        British Columbia / Kaite Goldsworthy.

(My Canada)
ISBN 978-1-77071-864-7 (bound).
ISBN 978-1-77071-865-4 (pbk.)

        1. British Columbia--Juvenile literature. I. Title. II. Series: My
Canada (Calgary, Alta.)

FC3811.2.G65 2013   j971.1   C2013-902391-7

Printed in the United States of America in North Mankato, Minnesota
1 2 3 4 5 6 7 8 9 0   17 16 15 14 13

052013
WEP040413

Project Coordinator: Megan Cuthbert
Art Director: Terry Paulhus

Weigl acknowledges Getty Images as the primary image
supplier for this title.

We acknowledge the financial support of the Government
of Canada through the Canada Book Fund for our
publishing activities.

Contents

3

This is British Columbia. It was named after the Columbia River. The river starts in British Columbia.

4

This is the shape of British Columbia. British Columbia is between Alberta and the Pacific Ocean.

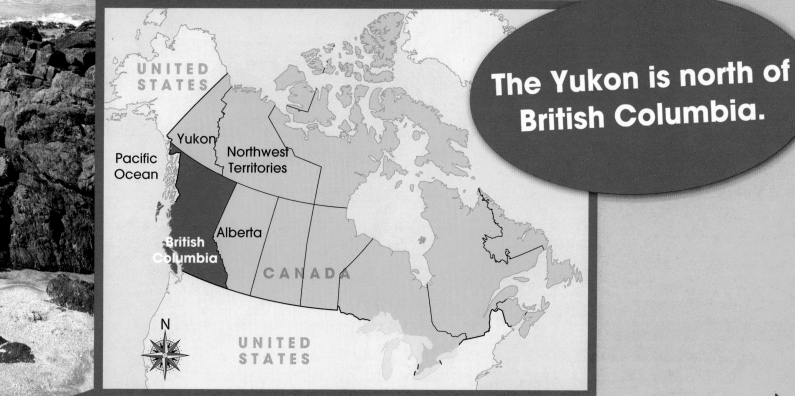

UNITED STATES

Yukon

Pacific Ocean

Northwest Territories

Alberta

British Columbia

CANADA

N

UNITED STATES

The Yukon is north of British Columbia.

7

Victoria is the capital city of British Columbia. It is known for its beautiful gardens.

Victoria has the tallest totem pole in the world.

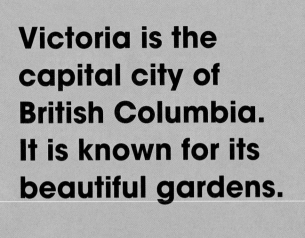

Gold was found in British Columbia in 1858 and 1862. People came from all around the world to look for gold.

Many towns, such as Barkerville, were built when people came to find gold.

The province's coat of arms has a shield with the flag of British Columbia on it. A lion wearing a crown sits at the top. A stag and ram are on each side of the shield.

A stag is a male deer. Only male deer grow antlers.

This is the flag of British Columbia. At the bottom of British Columbia's flag is a sun. At the top is the flag of Great Britain.

The blue and white wavy stripes on the flag stand for the mountains and water in the province.

Pacific dogwood is British Columbia's flower. It grows along the coast of the province.

The official animal of British Columbia is the spirit bear. Spirit bears are a kind of black bear that have white fur.

17

British Columbia has many large forests. Trees are used for wood, lumber, and paper.

Canada's largest tree is on Vancouver Island.

Many people visit the city of Vancouver every year. Vancouver is close to the ocean and the mountains.

The city is surrounded by water on three sides. People can go sailing and boating on the water.

BRITISH COLUMBIA FACTS

These pages provide detailed information that expands on the interesting facts found in the book. They are intended to be used by adults as a learning support to help young readers round out their knowledge of each province and territory in the *My Canada* series.

Pages 4–5

Queen Victoria chose the name British Columbia in 1858, including 'British' to emphasize that it was part of the British Empire. British Columbia is 944,735 square kilometres in area and is home to approximately 4.4 million people. The province has several mountain ranges, including the Coast Mountains, the Rockies, and Purcells.

Pages 6–7

British Columbia is the most western Canadian province and is bordered by the Pacific Ocean. British Columbia has a number of islands. The largest is Vancouver Island. British Columbia is bordered by Washington State, Idaho, and Montana to the south, and the state of Alaska to the northwest. The Yukon and Northwest Territories are directly north.

Pages 8–9

Victoria is located on Vancouver Island. It has a population of about 363,000. The city has the mildest climate in Canada. Victoria is known as the City of Gardens because of its beautiful flowers and long growing season. The totem pole in Beacon Hill Park stands nearly 39 metres tall. It was erected in 1956 and is carved from a cedar tree.

Pages 10–11

Approximately 30,000 people arrived in British Columbia to look for gold during the Fraser River Gold Rush. This great influx led to the area being declared a colony by Great Britain in 1858. Barkerville was the centre of the Cariboo Gold Rush in 1862. At the time, it was the biggest North American town west of Chicago and north of San Francisco. The town has been reconstructed and is now a tourist attraction.

Pages 12–13

Above British Columbia's shield is the Royal Crest, a lion standing on a crown. The lion wears a dogwood collar, the official flower of the province. The stag and ram represent the former colonies of Vancouver Island and British Columbia. Dogwood flowers surround the motto, which means "splendour without diminishment."

Pages 14–15

The Union Jack at the top of British Columbia's flag represents the origins of the province as a British colony. The blue and white wavy lines represent the Pacific Ocean and Rocky Mountains, and the setting sun represents the province's western location. The flag was officially adopted in 1960.

Pages 16–17

The Pacific dogwood grows up to 15 metres tall. It has small, white flowers in the spring and autumn. It also produces bitter, red berries. About 1,300 spirit bears live in British Columbia. They are found mostly on the central and north coast. The spirit bear is born with white fur. Approximately 1 in 40 black bears are spirit bears.

Pages 18–19

Forestry is a large part of British Columbia's economy. About one-fifth of the softwood lumber in Canada is from the province. Canada's largest tree is known as the Cheewhat Giant. It is a western red cedar and stands 56 metres tall and 6 metres wide. It grows in the Pacific Rim National Park Reserve on Vancouver Island.

Pages 20–21

The city of Vancouver has a population of approximately 603,500. Nearly nine million people visit Vancouver every year. To the north of the city is the Burrard Inlet, to the west is the Pacific Ocean's Strait of Georgia, and south is the Fraser River. The Coast Mountains overlook the city. The city is a popular location for outdoor activities.

KEY WORDS

Research has shown that as much as 65 percent of all written material published in English is made up of 300 words. These 300 words cannot be taught using pictures or learned by sounding them out. They must be recognized by sight. This book contains 61 common sight words to help young readers improve their reading fluency and comprehension. This book also teaches young readers several important content words, such as proper nouns. These words are paired with pictures to aid in learning and improve understanding.

Page	Sight Words First Appearance
4	after, in, is, it, named, river, starts, the, this, was
7	and, between, of
8	city, for, has, its, world
11	all, around, as, came, find, found, from, look, many, people, such, to, were, when
12	a, are, at, each, on, side, with
13	grow, only
15	mountains, water, white
16	along
17	animal, have, kind, that
19	large, paper, trees, used
20	by, can, close, come, every, go, three, year

Page	Content Words First Appearance
4	British Columbia
7	Alberta, Pacific Ocean, shape, United States, Yukon
8	gardens, totem pole, Victoria
11	Barkerville, gold, towns
12	coat of arms, crown, flag, lion, province, ram, shield, stag, top
13	antlers, deer
15	bottom, Great Britain, stripes, sun
16	coast, flower, Pacific dogwood
17	black bear, fur, spirit bear
19	Canada, forests, lumber, Vancouver Island, wood
20	ocean, sides, Vancouver

WEBSITES

To learn more about British Columbia, visit these websites.

Hello BC
http://www.hellobc.com

British Columbia Facts
http://www.gov.bc.ca/bcfacts/

KidZone
http://www.kidzone.ws/geography/bc/index.htm